Other Titles by this Author:

Fruits and Veggies in the Garden: Children Explain How Their Plants Grow | English
Frutas y Vegetales in el Jardín: Los Niños Explican Cómo Crecen Sus Plantas | Spanish with English Translation
I Spy Vegetables: A Seek and Find Early Science and Math Experience | English
Espío Vegetales: Una Experiencia de Buscar y Encontrar en las Ciencias y las Matemáticas Tempranas | Spanish and English
I Spy Fruit: A Seek and Find Early Science and Math Experience | English
Espío Frutas: Una Experiencia de Buscar y Encontrar en las Ciencias y las Matemáticas Tempranas | Spanish & English
We Eat Food That's Fresh: A Children's Picture Book about Tasting New Foods | English - 2nd Ed.
Probamos Comidas Nuevas: Un Chef Introduce Alimentos Saludables de Maneras Differentes a los Niños | Spanish & English
We Love the Company: A Children's Book about Table Manners | English - 2nd Ed. (Available in Spanish)
Fruits & Veggies Making Faces: A Children's Picture Book About Feelings, Emotions, and Self-Expression | English
Moving with Colors and Shapes: A Physically Interactive Early Math and Science-Based Children's Picture Book | English
Moviéndose con los Colores y las Formas | Spanish & English
Bouger Avec les Couleurs et les Formes | French & English

Visit AbridgeClub.com for more titles.

About the Author:

Angela Ayon (Russ-Ayon) resides in Long Beach, California, with her family. She is an author, keynote speaker, producer, and trainer on the subject of early childhood development, as well as the owner of the Russ InVision Company children's record label. Her company boasts over $1.5 million in sales, has been presented with nine early childhood music awards of excellence, and is represented by school suppliers nationwide. Her specialty is engaging young children in interactive song and dance using fine and gross motor activities that promote interactive learning, inspire imaginative play, help build brain pathways, and bridge educational gaps.

Translation by: Nancy Lopez-Hernandez   **Photo Editor:** Irina Mirskaya

Ayon It Publishing, a Russ InVision Company
Long Beach, CA 90808
E-mail: info@abridgeclub.com   www.AbridgeClub.com

ISBN: 978-1-958627-93-8
Spanish & English IngramSpark Paperback - 2nd edition

Espío frutas.

I spy fruit.

Espío frutas que son rojas.

I spy fruit that is red.

Espío frutas que son anaranjadas.

I spy fruit that is orange.

Espío fruta que es amarilla.

I spy fruit that is yellow.

Espío frutas que son verdes.

I spy fruit that is green.

Espío fruta que es azul.

I spy fruit that is blue.

Espío frutas que son moradas.

I spy fruit that is purple.

Espío frutas en un patrón.

I spy fruit in a pattern.

Espío frutas que se ven iguales.

I spy fruit that looks the same.

Espío fruta que se ve diferente.

I spy fruit that looks different.

Espío frutas que están clasificadas.

I spy fruit that is sorted.

Espío frutas en forma de círculos.

I spy fruit in the shape of circles.

Espío frutas en forma de cuadrados.

I spy fruit in the shape of squares.

Espío fruta en forma de triángulos.

I spy fruit in the shape of triangles.

Espío fruta en forma de estrellas.

I spy fruit in the shape of stars.

Espío frutas en forma de corazones.

I spy fruit in the shape of hearts.

Espío fruta en forma de gajos.

I spy fruit in the shape of wedges.

Espío segmentos de frutas.

I spy fruit segments.

Espío fruta que está madura.

I spy fruit that is ripe.

Espío fruta colgando alto y fruta colgando bajo.

I spy fruit hanging high and fruit hanging low.

Espío fruta que está pelada.

I spy fruit that is peeled.

Espío fruta que está seca.

I spy fruit that is dried.

Espío fruta que está enlatada.

I spy fruit that is canned.

Espío fruta que está fresca
y fruta que está pudriéndose.

I spy fruit that is fresh and fruit that is rotting.

Espío frutas que están congeladas.

I spy fruit that is frozen.

Espío fruta que se ha descongelado.

I spy fruit that has thawed.

Espío frutas flotando encima
y frutas que se hundieron al fondo.

I spy fruit floating on top and fruit that sank to the bottom.

Espío frutas que son reales
y frutas que son de mentira.

I spy fruit that is real and fruit that is pretend.

Espío jugos de fruta.

I spy fruit juices.

Espío frutas que están listas para comer.

I spy fruit that is ready to eat.

Consejos para la Lectura

Encuentren formas de conectar lo que están leyendo con un tema, experimento, actividad, y cualquier otro aspecto de la vida de un niño. Denle a los niños tiempo, espacio, y materiales para explorar por su cuenta.

- Ayuden a los niños a identificar las frutas.
- Hagan descubrimientos más allá de lo indicado en cada página. Busquen similitudes y diferencias en posiciones, formas, colores, tamaños, texturas, y otras características.
- Aprovechen cada oportunidad para contar.
- Examinen, diseccionen, y estudien frutas reales. Comiencen usando los cinco sentidos. Comparen la fruta real con la fruta falsa.
- Proporcionen implementos de escritura para que los niños puedan escribir un diario, registrar sus hallazgos,
o dibujar, incluso si están garabateando.
- Hagan un diario fotográfico de experiencias con las frutas.
- Hablen de las muchas formas en que se pueden preparar y disfrutar las frutas.
- Encuentren formas divertidas para interpretar palabras físicamente, como *círculo, cuadrado, alto, bajo, arriba, abajo, flotar, hundir, congelar, derretir,* etc.
- Repasen cómo la jardinería o seguir una receta implica una secuencia de eventos. Proporcionen ayudas visuales, como tarjetas que se puedan organizar en un orden lógico.
- Expongan a los niños a la terminología STEM, señales
de posición y dirección, y palabras de vocabulario más complejas todos los días.
- Canten y muévanse a unas canciones con palabras y conceptos de vocabulario STEM, o inventen una canción.

- Involucren a los niños en un proyecto de arte sobre frutas: coloreen, pinten, moldeen plastilina, estampen, corten y peguen, tejan, hagan libros a mano, etc.
- Presenten y experimenten con actividades STEM inspiradas por el libro, como clasificar, hundir/flotar, congelar/descongelar, fresco/podrido, causa/efecto, hacer patrones, mezclar colores, segmentar, real/falso, etc. (con la supervisión de un adulto).
- Planten un jardín simple adentro o afuera. Aprendan del proceso, luego cosechen, preparen, y coman lo que cultiven.
- Organicen una prueba de sabor. Hagan una encuesta. Registren gráficamente y muestren fotos y resultados.
- Las actividades y los experimentos que utilicen alimentos deberían terminar en probar los alimentos, si son comestibles, y no deben ser un desperdicio.
- Continúen explorando la ciencia de los seres vivos, como las plantas, los insectos que se encuentran alrededor de las plantas, los animales que comen plantas y los nutrientes esenciales proveidos por la fruta para el cuerpo humano.
- Construyan sobre los principios y las leyes científicás físicas básicas a través de la exploración práctica, por ejemplo cómo se mueven las cosas (hundir o flotar), cómo las cosas cambian de forma (de hielo a agua), y cómo se clasifican las cosas por características físicas.

Courtesy of AbridgeClub.com   ©2020 Russ InVision Co.

Reading Tips

Find ways to connect what you are reading to a theme, experiment, activity, and any other aspects of a child's life. Give children time, space, and materials to explore on their own.

- Help children identify fruit.
- Make discoveries beyond what is stated on each page. Look for similarities and differences in positions, shapes, colors, sizes, textures, and other characteristics.
- Take every opportunity to count.
- Examine, dissect, and study real fruit. Begin by using all five senses. Compare real fruit to fake fruit.
- Provide writing implements so the children can journal, record findings, or draw, even if they are scribbling.
- Make a photo journal of experiences with fruit.
- Discuss the many ways fruit can be prepared and enjoyed.
- Find fun ways to physically interpret words, such as *circle, square, high, low, top, bottom, float, sink, freeze, melt,* etc.
- Review how gardening or following a recipe involves a sequence of events. Provide visual aids, such as cards that can be arranged in a logical order.
- Expose children to STEM terminology, positional and directional cues, and more complex vocabulary words every day.
- Sing and move to songs with STEM vocabulary words and concepts, or make up a song.

- Involve children in an art project about fruit: color, paint, mold clay, stamp, cut and paste, weave, make books by hand, etc.
- Introduce and experiment with STEM activities inspired by the book, such as sorting, sink/float, freeze/thaw, fresh/decay, cause/effect, making patterns, mixing colors, segmenting, real/fake, etc. (with adult supervision).
- Plant a simple garden indoors or out. Learn from the process, then harvest, prepare, and eat what you grow.
- Organize a taste test. Take a poll. Chart and display photos and results.
- Food activities and experiments should lead to the tasting of food, if it's edible, and should not be wasteful.
- Continue to explore the science of living things, such as plants, insects found around plants, animals that eat plants, and the essential nutrients supplied by fruit for the human body.
- Build on basic physical scientific principles and laws through hands-on exploration, such as how things move (sink or float), how things change forms (ice to water), and how things are sorted by physical characteristics.

Preguntas Abiertas • Open-ended Questions

Aquí hay ejemplos de indagaciones abiertas que pueden fomentar la observación y alimentar la curiosidad innata de un niño mientras navegan por las páginas juntos:

Here are some examples of open-ended inquiry that can encourage observation and nurture a child's innate curiosity as you navigate through the pages together:

1. ¿De qué crees que se trata este libro?
2. ¿Qué sabes de la fruta?
3. ¿Cuál es tu fruta favorita/menos favorita? ¿Por qué?
4. ¿Cómo son iguales/diferentes?
5. ¿Por qué crees que es importante comer fruta?
6. ¿Qué notas en esta página?
7. Describe lo que ve.
8. ¿Cómo sabes que es un plátano/una pera/un kiwi/ etc.?
9. ¿Cómo sabes si la fruta es real o falsa?
10. ¿Cómo comerías esta fruta?
11. ¿Cómo sabes cuando la fruta está lista para comer?
12. ¿Por qué crees que la fruta es tan colorida?
13. ¿Qué sabes sobre las semillas/raíces/hojas /tallos/ cáscaras/piel?
14. ¿Por qué crees que la fruta tiene semillas/raíces/ hojas/ tallos/piel/cáscara?
15. ¿Cómo sabes cual semilla/hoja/tallo/cáscara/piel va con cual fruta?
16. ¿Cómo crees que las semillas se convierten en frutas?
17. Muéstrame cómo crece una planta usando tu cuerpo.
18. ¿Por qué crees que las plantas necesitan tierra/agua/ sol?
19. ¿Cómo se clasifica la fruta?
20. ¿Cómo puedes saber cuántos hay?
21. ¿Por qué crees que son de diferentes tamaños?
22. ¿Por qué crees que la fruta flota/se hunde/se seca / se congela/se descongela?
23. ¿Cómo crees que funciona esa herramienta?
24. ¿Cómo puedes obtener más información sobre eso?

1. What do you think this book is about?
2. What do you know about fruit?
3. What is your favorite/least favorite fruit? Why?
4. How are these the same/different?
5. Why do you think eating fruit is important?
6. What do you notice on this page?
7. Describe what you see.
8. How do you know that's a banana/pear/kiwi/etc.?
9. How do you know if the fruit is real or pretend?
10. How would you eat this fruit?
11. How do you know when the fruit is ready to eat?
12. Why do you think fruit is so colorful?
13. What do you know about seeds/roots/leaves/ stems/peels/skin?
14. Why do you think fruit has seeds/roots/leaves/ stems/skin/peels?
15. How do you know which seed/leaf/stem/peel/skin goes to which fruit?
16. How do you think seeds grow into fruit?
17. Show me how a plant grows using your body.
18. Why do you think plants need dirt/water/sun?
19. How is the fruit sorted?
20. How can you tell how many there are?
21. Why do you think they are different sizes?
22. Why do you think fruit floats/sinks/dries/freezes/ thaws?
23. How do you think that tool works?
24. How can you find out more about it?

Courtesy of AbridgeClub.com   ©2020 Russ InVision Co.

www.ingramcontent.com/pod-product-compliance
Lightning Source LLC
Chambersburg PA
CBHW041558120626
46551CB00002B/256